REBEL ✛ RESCUE

REBEL ✛ RESCUE

Transform Your Child from Defiant & Lazy to Compliant & Driven

K.D. SIMS

INTRODUCTION

In a world that's constantly evolving, parenting has never been more complex. With our busy schedules, the influx of technology, and the pressure to raise well-rounded, successful children, many parents find themselves facing a unique set of challenges. Among these, perhaps the most common and frustrating is dealing with defiant children who resist authority and lazy kids who seem disinterested in putting in the effort. But what if I told you that understanding the underlying reasons behind these behaviors can transform not only how you interact with your child but also foster a more harmonious family environment?

Welcome to *"Rebel Rescue"* where we dive deep into practical methods that help shift your child's defiant behavior and lazy attitudes toward listening and working. This guide goes beyond mere discipline techniques; it explores a holistic approach that prioritizes connection, empathy, and empowerment. By recognizing that defiance often stems from underlying emotions—fear, frustration, or a sometimes overwhelming sense of independence—we can engage in more meaningful conversations that pave the way for cooperation. Similarly, laziness can often be misdiagnosed; instead of mere lack of motivation, it could be a sign of overwhelm, confusion, or a simple desire for fun.

Throughout this book, we will explore 15 comprehensive strategies designed to equip you with the tools necessary to unlock the potential in your defiant or seemingly lazy child. These strategies are not merely quick fixes; they are rooted in research and best practices in child development, psychology, and educational theory. The aim is to empower not just your children but you as a parent, providing you with the knowledge and confidence to engage with your kids in a way that fosters growth and understanding.

From understanding what drives defiant behavior to setting up systems that replace laziness with motivation, we will systematically approach each aspect of these challenging situations. We'll discuss the importance of establishing a positive environment and the power of effective communication that resonates with children of all ages. You'll learn the art of negotiating with your child, turning confrontations into constructive dialogues.

TABLE OF CONTENTS

Chapter 1: Understanding Defiance - The Root Causes of Resistance

Defiance in Kids: Cracking the Code

Ah, defiance. It's that moment every parent dreads: one minute, your little dynamo is happily engrossed in Lego towers, and the next, they're throwing a mini tantrum, declaring "No!" like it's their favorite word. Talk about a twist in the plot. But why does defiance rear its head so frequently? Let's unravel this perplexing riddle and see that often, those rebellious stirrings run much deeper than simple stubbornness.

The Colorful Spectrum of Defiance

You see, defiance isn't one-size-fits-all. It dances across a spectrum, each hue representing different motivations. On one side, we have the fiery little ones with strong-willed personalities. These kiddos thrive on making their own choices, fiercely guarding their independence like a dragon protecting its treasure. They're the mini-mavericks, and to them, "No" is an anthem of self-assertion.

On the flip side, there are those who might wield defiance as a shield against an emotional storm. When things get overwhelming—think of a long school day and homework looming—it's easy for a child to lash out, not because they're lazy or disobedient, but because they're navigating a whirlwind of feelings. So, understanding what lies beneath the surface can transform frustration into connection.

Emotional Triggers: The Hidden Culprit

Let's dive into the emotional undercurrents. Kids are still figuring out the tricky tapestry of their feelings. When emotions like anger, sadness, or frustration bubble to the surface, defiance can follow. Picture this: your child arrives home after a hectic day, and when asked to tackle homework, they erupt. It's not that they hate learning; they're simply drowning in overwhelm. Tuning into these emotional triggers is key to defusing the situation, allowing us to dive deeper into understanding.

Nurturing Emotional Intelligence: Your Toolkit

So how do we help our kiddos manage their emotional eruptions? Here are some gems:

- **Talk It Out**: Make it a routine! Chat about feelings like they're no big deal. Ask them, "How did that make you feel?" Build a space where expression is celebrated.

- **Validate**: When your little one shares their feelings, say things like, "It's totally okay to feel that way." Offer words to help them articulate what's swirling inside, turning chaos into clarity.

- **Mindfulness Magic**: Teach them to breathe deep or visualize a peaceful scene. These skills can help them hit the brakes when emotions are racing.

The Communication Breakdown: Left in the Noise

Now let's tackle another sneaky culprit behind defiance—a breakdown in communication. Kids often feel like they're talking to a wall. When parents bark orders without context, resentment simmers. It's like being handed a mystery puzzle without the picture on the box. Engaging in real, open conversations can make all the difference.

Effective Communication Strategies: Bridge the Gap

How can we bridge this communication divide? Let's explore:

- **Active Listening**: Put down the phone, turn to your child, and really listen. Give them your full attention. No interruptions, just pure, heartfelt listening.

- **Clear Expectations**: A sprinkle of clarity goes a long way! When you explain why certain rules exist, it transforms directives into digestible nuggets of wisdom. Phrase requests positively— instead of "Don't leave your toys scattered," say "Let's put your toys away together!"

- **Choice, Please**: Give them some say in the matter. Instead of saying, "Clean your room," try, "Would you prefer to clean your room now or after snack?" Empowerment goes a long way in easing defiance.

The Role of Environment: Home Sweet ... Tumultuous?

Let's not forget our surroundings! A chaotic or unstable home can feel like a storm cloud hovering over kids, making them crave control. Kids flourish in structured, predictable environments—think lush gardens where they can thrive!

Creating a Nest of Security

What are some ways to establish this nurturing environment?

- **Set Routines**: Routines create comfort and stability. They're like the gentle rhythm of a lullaby that helps soothe anxiety.

- **Designate Spaces**: Create cozy corners for specific activities—homework zones, play areas, or relaxation spots. This makes tasks feel manageable, lessening the overwhelm that often leads to resistance.

A Quest for Independence

At the heart of defiance lies a powerful desire: independence. As children grow, they crave the freedom to explore their autonomy. It's not about pushing boundaries for the sake of chaos; it's a crucial part of developing into their own people.

Nurturing Their Growing Wings

Here's how to balance guidance with independence:

- **Involve Them in Decisions**: Let them have a say! Whether it's choosing the weekend adventure or selecting the dinner menu, involving them in family decisions can be incredibly empowering.

- **Goal Setting Together**: Encourage them to help set their own goals, be it for chores or schoolwork. This grants them ownership over their responsibilities, transforming burdens into achievements.

Wrapping Up: The Road Ahead

So, my fellow parents, understanding the complexities behind your child's defiance is like flipping on a light in a dark room. Recognizing the emotional triggers, communication misfires, environmental impacts, and the yearning for independence can shift frustrations into effective strategies.

And just around the corner, in the next chapter, we'll tackle the intriguing phenomenon of laziness—what it really means, how to tackle it, and the art of motivation without force. With newfound insights into emotions, communication, and fostering independence, you'll be well-equipped to guide your child toward becoming the motivated, cooperative superstar they're meant to be. Buckle up; the journey promises to be both enlightening and enriching!

Chapter 2: Melting Laziness - What Makes Kids Tick?

Let's face it: we've all encountered those moments when our kids seem to hit the snooze button on life—ignoring responsibilities and procrastinating on tasks they once enjoyed. This chapter will explore the phenomenon of laziness in children, demystifying its causes and offering actionable strategies to motivate them without the inevitable power struggles.

Understanding Laziness

Laziness is often dismissed as mere unwillingness to work or participate, but it's essential to look beyond the surface. When a child refuses to engage in activities—whether it's homework, chores, or hobbies—there's often a deeper reason. It's important to differentiate between genuine laziness and what might appear to be laziness but stems from other influences like fatigue, lack of interest, anxiety, or even learning difficulties.

The Many Faces of Laziness

1. Physical Fatigue

Kids lead busy lives. Between school, extracurricular activities, and social interactions, they can become physically and mentally exhausted. Tired children may lack the energy to complete tasks that once excited them.

- **Encourage Regular Breaks:** Heavy workloads can drain energy. Suggest short breaks for rest and rejuvenation. Kids may benefit from the Pomodoro Technique, where they work for 25 minutes and then take a 5-minute break.
- **Evaluate Activity Levels:** Check if your child is over-scheduled. Too many activities can lead to burnout, resulting in a lack of enthusiasm.

2. Overwhelm and Anxiety

Sometimes, laziness masks deeper feelings of overwhelm or anxiety. When faced with daunting tasks—like a large school project or cleaning their room—children may freeze, appearing lazy when, in fact, they're feeling paralyzed by negativity.

Strategies for Addressing Overwhelm:

- **Chunk Tasks:** Help them break large projects into smaller, manageable parts. Instead of "clean your room," say, "Let's start by picking up clothes for 10 minutes and then pause." This prevents feelings of being overwhelmed.
- **Encourage Goal Setting:** Encourage small, achievable goals such as completing just one section of homework at a time. Celebrate each success to build confidence.

3. Lack of Interest or Passion

Some kids may express laziness due to a lack of interest in the task at hand. Forced engagement in activities that hold no meaning can lead to disinterest and reluctance to participate.

Strategies for Building Interest:

- **Engage in Dialogue:** Instead of dictating what they must do, ask about their interests. What do they enjoy? How can these interests be incorporated into their responsibilities? For instance, if they love art, let them create a colorful chore chart.
- **Create Opportunities for Choice:** Giving children options promotes autonomy. Instead of saying, "Do your homework," ask, "Would you prefer to do math or reading first?" Letting them choose makes them feel more in control.

Investing in Motivational Strategies

Now that we understand some root causes of laziness, let's turn our attention toward intrinsic motivation—the power of fostering a sense of drive from within. Here are some strategies that focus on building this motivation.

1. Set Clear Expectations

Children need a clear understanding of what is expected of them. The absence of defined tasks can result in ambiguity, leading to procrastination.

- **Concrete Guidelines:** Be specific about what you want them to do. Instead of a vague, "Clean your room," try "Please pick up your toys and put your clothes in the laundry."

2. Establish Routines

Consistency is key in creating an efficient environment. Children thrive on routines. They feel safe and know what to expect, which minimizes resistance.

- **Morning Routines:** Set a clear and engaging morning routine, turning it into a fun family activity. Listen to music, set a timer for each task, and watch how they quickly adapt.
- **Evening Check-Ins:** Each evening, hold a family meeting to discuss what tasks you want everyone to accomplish the next day.

3. Positive Reinforcement

Using positive reinforcement is one of the most effective ways to encourage desired behavior. Children respond amazingly to rewards, be it verbal praise or tangible rewards.

Implementing a Reward System:

- **Sticker Charts:** Create a sticker chart for tasks completed, offering small rewards for reaching milestones, such as a family outing.
- **Celebrate Victories, Big and Small:** Praise efforts, regardless of the outcome. A simple "I noticed you tried hard on your project" can motivate them to engage in the next task with enthusiasm.

4. Encourage Reflection

Teach your child the benefits of self-reflection. After completing a task (even if there was initial resistance), have them think about how they felt during and after completing it.

- **Reflection Questions:** Ask questions after a task is finished, such as "How did you feel when you finished your homework?" or "What was your favorite part of cleaning your room?"

The Role of Play

Play should never be underestimated in child development. Incorporating play into tasks can turn boring responsibilities into enjoyable challenges that encourage engagement.

- **Gamify Tasks:** Turn chores into games. Have them race against time or create a scoring system where they earn points for each task completed within a time frame.
- **Creative Homework Approaches:** Encourage creativity in homework. For example, if they're assigned a report, encourage them to present it as a skit or artwork.

Modeling Enthusiasm

Children learn by observing. Model the enthusiasm you would like to see in your child. When they see you working with energy or tackling tasks with a positive attitude, they are more likely to mimic that behavior.

- **Share Your Tasks:** Involve them in your chores. Share the joy of keeping the house tidy by saying, "Look how great this room looks when we work together!"

- **Show Your Work:** Share your own challenges and triumphs over responsibilities. It makes the experience relatable and emphasizes that everyone faces challenges but benefits from working together.

Fostering Persistence and Resilience

Lastly, training your child in persistence and resilience is crucial. Life will always throw challenges their way, and teaching them to navigate through smooth and rough waters builds character and work ethic.

- **Encouragement to Persist:** Remind your child that some tasks might be tough, but persistence often leads to satisfaction. Apply the philosophy that "practice makes progress" rather than expecting perfection.
- **Normalize Setbacks:** Teach them that everyone experiences setbacks. It's how we respond to them that matters.

Conclusion of Chapter 2

In embracing the complexities of why children may seem "lazy," we can better approach these behaviors with understanding and compassion. By employing these strategies, you'll not only motivate your child but also empower them to tackle future responsibilities with confidence and enthusiasm. The next chapter will focus on building effective communication lines that encourage listening and understanding, establishing a foundation for further connection.

Chapter 3: The Power of Connection - Building Trust with Your Child

Building a Connection with Your Child: The Key to Cooperation and Motivation

Creating a strong bond with your child isn't just a nice idea; it's one of the most powerful strategies out there for encouraging cooperation and motivating them to listen. Imagine transforming moments of defiance and lethargy into enthusiasm and engagement! In this chapter, we'll dive into the many ways you can cultivate a loving, trustworthy relationship with your child, making them more inclined to collaborate with you rather than push back.

The Importance of Connection: Why It Matters

Before we launch into specific strategies, let's pause and consider why connection is essential. Think of it as the bedrock of healthy relationships. Connection nurtures emotional security, mutual respect, and, most importantly, open communication. When kids feel that special bond with their parents, they're more likely to trust you and follow your guidance. The benefits are palpable—lower levels of defiance and increased emotional resilience, self-worth, and overall well-being.

Why Trust is Crucial:

- **Emotional Safety**: When kids feel safe emotionally, they're more likely to share their feelings freely instead of flipping into defiant mode or retreating into a slump.

- **Willingness to Listen**: Trust creates a solid foundation where children are more apt to listen to you—knowing you genuinely care about their interests and well-being fosters active engagement.

- **Increased Cooperation**: Kids who feel valued and connected are naturally more inclined to cooperate. They recognize their actions play a role in the family dynamic, which helps mitigate feelings of isolation.

Building Trust Through Active Engagement

Active engagement is all about being present and attentive when you spend time with your child. Here are some heartfelt ways to show love and foster connection, opening the door to meaningful conversations:

1. Quality One-on-One Time

Life gets busy, but carving out regular, distraction-free time with your child is priceless. This is when you can truly connect and immerse yourselves in their world.

- **Plan Activities Together**: Whether it's biking around the neighborhood, playing a board game, or getting crafty, choose activities that spark their joy. The goal? Make it fun and exciting for them!

- **Be Present**: Silence those notifications! Put down your phone to show you're all in. This reinforces emotional ties and assures them their feelings are important.

2. Show Genuine Interest

Take a genuine interest in what makes your child tick—their dreams, fears, and everything in between.

- **Ask Open-Ended Questions**: Get the conversation flowing with questions like, "What was the best part of your day?" or "What made you feel proud today?" This invites them to express themselves and deepens your connection.

- **Listen Actively**: When your child talks, listen like it's the most important story ever. Reflect back what they've said to show you care. For example, "It sounds like you were really disappointed when your friend didn't invite you to that party."

Establishing Emotional Availability

Being emotionally available means tuning into your child's feelings and responding appropriately. Kids are incredibly perceptive; they can pick up on your emotional state, and if you're distracted, it can erode the trust you've built.

- **Validate Their Feelings**: When your child expresses emotions like anger or sadness, acknowledge those feelings. Saying, "It's completely normal to feel upset about that" can help them feel heard and understood.

- **Share Your Emotions**: Don't be afraid to show your own feelings too! Sharing your challenges can foster solidarity. It humanizes you in their eyes, making it easier for them to connect and trust you.

Enhancing Communication Skills

Effective communication is at the heart of reinforcing trust and connection. Improving these skills not only benefits your family dynamic but also sets a powerful example for your child.

1. Speak with Empathy

Use language that resonates with your child's experiences. Speaking empathetically opens doors and encourages cooperation while minimizing defensiveness.

- **Adjust Your Language**: Match your communication style to your child's level of understanding. Ditch the condescending tone; complex vocab might alienate them instead of winning their hearts.

- **Use "I" Statements**: Instead of saying, "You never finish your homework," try "I feel anxious when your homework isn't done." This promotes understanding and avoids a combative atmosphere.

2. Non-Verbal Cues Matter

Don't forget—communication isn't just about words! Your body language speaks volumes.

- **Maintain Eye Contact**: Lock eyes when conversing. It signals that they have your undivided attention and shows you're truly engaged.

- **Positive Body Language**: Lean in, nod, and use open gestures. Avoid crossing your arms or fidgeting; those can signal disinterest or irritation.

Creating a Safe Space for Openness

Establishing a safe space makes all the difference. It encourages kids to express their thoughts and feelings without fear of judgment.

- **Set Ground Rules**: Develop guidelines around discussing feelings—like respecting all emotions expressed. No dismissing feelings as silly or unimportant!

- **Empower Problem-Solving**: Instead of jumping in with solutions, let your child brainstorm how to handle challenges. This promotes autonomy and reflects that their opinions are valued.

The Role of Consistency

Building trust is a marathon, not a sprint. Consistency is key. Kids need to know you'll be there for them during both the sunny days and the stormy ones.

- **Follow Through on Promises**: If you say you'll spend time together or stick to a reward system, make sure to do it. Keeping your commitments reinforces reliability.

- **Regular Check-Ins**: Make it routine to check in about thoughts and feelings. This ongoing dialogue cultivates trust over time.

Fostering Independence While Staying Connected

While building that trust is critical, don't forget to encourage independence. Finding this balance helps children feel secure while developing self-reliance.

- **Encourage Autonomy**: Allow your child to make choices that affect them, like setting bedtime or picking out clothes. This fosters personal responsibility.

- **Guide Decision-Making**: Help them through decision-making without taking control. Let them weigh options and consider consequences—it's a crucial life lesson!

Conclusion of Chapter 3

Establishing a strong bond of trust and connection is vital for creating a cooperative atmosphere. Through active engagement, emotional availability, effective communication, and consistency, you're not just nurturing a relationship; you're instilling an intrinsic desire in your child to listen and participate. They'll feel secure in their connection with you, which acts as a protective barrier against defiance and laziness, making room for embracing responsibilities.

Next up, we'll delve into creating an environment that sets the stage for success—one that inspires both listening and hard work. Get ready for more tools to empower your family journey!

Chapter 4: Setting the Stage - Creating a Productive Environment

A productive environment is essential for fostering positive behaviors, such as listening and engaging in work. The physical and emotional atmosphere of your home greatly influences your child's ability to focus, listen, and complete tasks effectively. In this chapter, we will explore how to create an environment that not only minimizes distractions but also encourages your child to take initiative, develop good habits, and find joy in working toward their goals.

Understanding the Elements of a Productive Environment

Before we can create a productive environment, we need to identify the key elements that contribute to it. A productive environment is one that promotes focus, encourages responsibility, and builds a sense of belonging and safety. These elements include:

1. **Clutter-Free Space**: A tidy area helps children concentrate better. Clutter can be overwhelming and distracting, leading to feelings of frustration and avoidance.
2. **Comfort and Accessibility**: The space should be comfortable and organized, with easy access to materials they need for studying or chores.
3. **Defined Areas for Activities**: Designating specific areas for homework, chores, and play help children distinguish between different activities, reinforcing their focus during each task.

4.   **Positive Atmosphere**: The emotional tone of your home can significantly influence your child's mood and motivation. An atmosphere filled with encouragement, warmth, and understanding promotes better engagement.

Decluttering and Organizing Spaces

1. Start with a Clean Slate
The first step in creating a productive environment is decluttering. Take the time to involve your child in organizing their spaces. Here's how you can approach decluttering together:

- **Set a Date**: Choose a specific day to tackle the decluttering process. Make it a fun family day where everyone can contribute.
- **Sort Together**: Bring bins for sorting items into categories: keep, donate, and toss. This method can help your child make decisions about their belongings.
- **Create Space for Essentials**: Ensure that your child's workspace has only the items they need. Limit distractions by minimizing toys or unrelated items in study areas.

2. Organizing Supplies
Once you've cleared the clutter, it's time to organize supplies to ensure easy access. Invest in storage solutions that work for your family, such as:

- **Clear Bins or Baskets**: Label them for easy identification. Kids can quickly find what they need without frustration.
- **Desk Organizers**: For homework spaces, use trays or organizers to keep pens, markers, and notebooks easily accessible.

- **Color-Coding Systems**: Associate colors with subjects or tasks, allowing kids to grab materials quickly based on their assignments or activities.

Creating Dedicated Spaces for Different Activities

1. Homework Station
Your child should have a quiet, dedicated space for homework that is free from distractions. Consider these features for an effective homework station:

- **Desk and Comfortable Chair**: Ensure they have a well-lit desk with an ergonomic chair to promote good posture during study sessions.
- **Necessary Supplies**: Stock the space with all necessary supplies—pencils, paper, a calculator, etc.—to minimize interruptions when they need to get up for something.
- **Reduce Screen Time**: If possible, limit access to devices during studying (unless it's necessary for schoolwork). This helps to minimize distraction from notifications and social media.

2. Play and Creative Spaces
While studying and work are essential, allocating spaces for play and creativity is just as important. This balance prevents burnout and encourages literacy through play.

- **Designate a Play Area**: Allow your child a space for unstructured play, where they can freely explore their creativity without the potential for distractions that homework might bring.
- **Art Supplies Corner**: Create an area for art supplies that is easily accessible. Encourage your child to express their artistic talents, fostering both creativity and relaxation.

Enhancing Comfort and Focus

1. Lighting Matters
The lighting in a room can significantly affect mood and concentration. Ensure that your child's workspaces are well-lit:

- **Natural Light**: Whenever possible, choose spaces with ample natural light. Sunlight improves mood, productivity, and focus.
- **Task Lighting**: For evening study sessions or areas lacking natural light, use adjustable task lighting to avoid eye strain.

2. Temperature and Air Quality
The physical comfort of the environment is crucial for maintaining focus.

- **Temperature Control**: Ensure that workspaces are at a comfortable temperature—neither too hot nor too cold. Allow children to adjust these settings if possible by using fans or space heaters.
- **Fresh Air**: Spend time opening windows or using air purifiers to circulate fresh air. A well-ventilated space can improve mood and concentration.

The Emotional Environment: Creating a Safe and Supportive Space

While the physical setup is important, the emotional atmosphere can have a profound impact on productivity.

1. Encouraging and Positive Communication

- **Positive Reinforcement**: When your child completes tasks, acknowledge their efforts. Simple phrases like, "I am so proud of how you motivated yourself to finish your homework!" can build confidence and a sense of accomplishment.
- **Embrace Open Dialogue**: Make your home an emotionally safe space where children can discuss feelings without judgment. Reinforce their decisions and emotions as valid, building a foundation of respect.

2. Establishing Family Values

- **Create Family Goals**: Establish family values and responsibilities together. When kids know what's expected of them and feel part of a team, they are more inclined to participate willingly.
- **Display Family Achievements**: Create a dedicated space in the home to display family achievements, awards, and artwork to encourage positivity and a sense of belonging.

Setting Up Routines to Support Productivity

Routines provide structure, which is essential for children to thrive. Routines also establish expectations, reducing resistance. This is how you can implement effective routines in your home:

1. Visual Schedules

- **Daily Checklists**: Consider creating a visual schedule or checklist for your child's tasks. Children can follow along and check off items, which helps them take ownership over their responsibilities.

- **Morning and Evening Routines**: Build predictable structures for mornings and evenings, creating a seamless transition into the school day or winding down in the evening.

2. Celebrate Routines Together

Make daily routines feel like a family effort. Whether it's creating a bedtime routine that includes reading together or designing chores that allow collaboration, these moments encourage teamwork and foster connection.

Conclusion of Chapter 4

By establishing a productive environment, both physically and emotionally, you equip your child with the tools necessary for success. Whether it's through organizing spaces, enhancing comfort, or embracing supportive communication, you create a landscape where listening and hard work are celebrated. In the next chapter, we will explore effective communication strategies—how to speak so kids listen and how to engage in meaningful conversations that foster understanding and collaboration.

Chapter 5: Effective Communication - Speaking So Kids Listen

Effective communication is the cornerstone of any healthy relationship, especially between parents and children. The way we communicate with our kids can either foster an environment of cooperation or lead to misunderstandings and conflict. In this chapter, we will explore proven techniques to enhance your communication skills, ensuring that your child not only hears you but also understands and respects what you have to say.

The Foundations of Effective Communication

Before diving into strategies, it's critical to understand the foundations of effective communication. Building a solid framework is essential because how we communicate influences how messages are received.

1. **Clarity**: Clear and concise communication is vital. When our words are muddled or complex, children may become confused or tune out.

2. **Empathy**: Demonstrating empathy allows children to feel understood and valued, fostering a sense of safety when sharing their own thoughts and feelings.

3. **Active Listening**: Effective communication is a two-way street. Kids need to know they are being heard just as much as they need to listen to their parents.

Strategies for Clear and Effective Communication

1. Use Simple Language

Children process language differently than adults. Using simple and age-appropriate language can significantly impact their ability to comprehend your message.

- **Be Direct**: Avoid lengthy explanations that may confuse your child. Instead of saying, "I'd like you to consider the importance of keeping your room clean and how it can affect your overall organization," try expressing, "Please pick up your toys and clothes. It helps keep your room nice."

- **Break Down Instructions**: When giving multi-step instructions, break them down into manageable tasks. Instead of, "Clean your room, do your homework, and help with dinner," say, "First, let's pick up all the toys in your room."

2. Focus on Positive Language

The way your messages are framed can influence your child's behavior significantly. Positive language can empower children, while negative phrasing can create resistance.

- **Rephrase Negative Commands**: Instead of saying, "Don't leave your clothes on the floor," try, "Please put your clothes in the laundry basket." This shift encourages compliance by framing the request positively.

- **Highlight What They Did Right**: When addressing issues, start with specific praise followed by constructive feedback. For example, "I love how you cleaned your desk! Now let's work on organizing your books next."

Fostering Empathy Through Communication

1. Show Emotion

Authenticity fostered through emotional expression can help your child relate to you more deeply.

- **Share Your Feelings**: Use "I" statements to express feelings during discussions. For instance, "I feel worried when the homework isn't done because I want you to succeed." It allows you to express your emotions without placing blame.

- **Acknowledge Their Feelings**: When your child expresses frustration or sadness, validate those feelings by saying, "I understand that you feel frustrated about your homework; it can be tough sometimes." Acknowledging their emotions prompts them to express themselves more freely.

2. Use Reflective Listening

Reflective listening requires summarizing what your child says to ensure they feel understood, creating a base for open conversation.

- **Paraphrasing**: After your child speaks, paraphrase what they said. For example, "It sounds like you're feeling overwhelmed by your project. Would you like help?" This not only assures them you're listening but encourages them to elaborate if necessary.

Engaging in Active Listening

1. Give Full Attention

Active listening involves being present during conversations. Children need to feel that their words matter.

- **Remove Distractions**: When your child is speaking, set aside your phone or other distractions. Make eye contact to show genuine interest in what they're sharing.

- **Respond Appropriately**: Use verbal nods like "I see" or "Go on" to encourage them to keep talking. This creates an open dialogue and makes them feel heard.

2. Ask Open-Ended Questions

Open-ended questions propel conversations and encourage your child to express an array of thoughts and feelings.

- **Encourage Exploration**: Instead of asking, "Did you have a good day at school?" try, "What was the best part of your day?" This invites them to share more than a simple yes or no answer.

- **Facilitate Reflection**: Prompt your child with questions that inspire thought. Ask, "What do you think you could do differently next time?" to help them think critically about their experiences.

The Art of Negotiation

Sometimes, finding your child's compliance requires a bit of negotiation. Learning how to negotiate effectively can turn potential conflicts into collaborative discussions.

1. Present Choices Empowering your child with choices fosters a sense of control. It shifts the dynamic from one of authority to collaboration.

- **Offer Limited Options**: Instead of demanding compliance, present choices that allow your child to decide. For instance, "Would you like to do your homework now or after our snack?"

- **Incorporate Their Interests**: If possible, allow your child to choose how they want to tackle tasks. For example, "You can clean your room quickly, or we can set a timer and see how many tasks you can finish in 10 minutes."

2. Collaborative Goal-Setting

Involving your child in setting goals encourages accountability. Together, you can create expectations that make completing tasks easier.

- **Shared Responsibility**: Set goals with your child and ask them for input. For instance, "What do you think is a good goal for finishing your homework this week? How can we accomplish it?"

- **Check-Ins and Adjustments**: Once the goals are established, schedule regular check-ins to assess progress and adjust plans if necessary. This helps them learn to manage expectations and feel ownership over their tasks.

Encouraging a Dialogue, Not a Monologue

Parents often get caught in the pattern of delivering instructions or lectures without allowing children to voice their opinions. A dialogue is crucial for mutual understanding.

- **Seek Feedback**: After discussing an expectation or task, ask for your child's thoughts. "How do you feel about this plan? Is there anything you would want to change?"

- **Encourage Brainstorming**: Encourage your child to come up with solutions for their challenges. If they are reluctant to complete chores, ask, "Why do you think it's hard to start? How could we make it easier?"

Handling Conflict with Grace

Sometimes, discussions can lead to disagreements. The ability to communicate effectively during times of conflict is essential for long-term relationship health.

1. Stay Calm and Composed
As tensions rise, remain calm and composed. Your emotional regulation sets the tone for the conversation.

- **Take Breaks**: If a discussion becomes heated, suggest taking a break before revisiting the conversation. This gives both you and your child time to cool off, resulting in a more fruitful discussion later on.

- **Model Respectful Communication**: Use respectful language even when you disagree, demonstrating the importance of articulation and understanding during conflict resolution.

2. Focus on Solutions

During disagreements, steer the conversation toward productive solutions rather than dwelling on blame.

- **Collaborate on Solutions**: Ask questions like, "How can we solve this together?" or "What do you think we should do next?" This turns conflict into collaboration, allowing your child to feel they're an active participant.

Conclusion of Chapter 5

Effective communication opens doors to cooperation, allowing children to feel understood and respected. By employing clear language, demonstrating empathy, practicing active listening, and engaging in dialogue, you can significantly improve your relationship with your child. As we move forward to the next chapter, we will explore incentives and accountability—how to create a motivating system that encourages kids to take ownership of their work and responsibilities while fostering an environment of independence.

Chapter 6: Incentives and Accountability - Motivating Kids to Act

Incentives and accountability play crucial roles in motivating children to take responsibility for their actions. While it's easy to view incentives as mere rewards, they can actually serve as powerful tools for teaching children about consequences, encouraging good habits, and fostering a sense of responsibility. In this chapter, we will explore various strategies to create effective incentive systems and promote accountability, helping your child transition from a mindset of defiance or laziness to one of commitment and engagement.

Understanding Incentives and Their Impact

Incentives can take many forms; they don't always have to be materialistic. Recognizing what motivates your child is key in designing effective incentives. Here are some insights about incentives:

1. **Intrinsic vs. Extrinsic Motivation**:

    - **Intrinsic Motivation**: This comes from within the child. They engage in activities because they find them enjoyable or fulfilling.
    - **Extrinsic Motivation**: This is driven by external rewards, such as praise, stickers, or privileges. While extrinsic motivation can spur action, it's essential to cultivate intrinsic motivation for long-term engagement.

2. **Age-Appropriate Incentives**: What works for a toddler may not resonate with a teenager. Tailoring incentives to fit your child's age and maturity level helps to ensure effectiveness.

Designing Effective Incentive Systems

1. Create a Reward System

Reward systems can significantly boost motivation, especially when it comes to completing chores or homework. Here's how you can design one:

- **Sticker Charts**: For younger children, sticker charts can be an effective visual representation of accomplishments. Assign stickers for each completed task, and once a certain number is achieved, allow them to select a reward (like a fun outing).

- **Point systems**: Develop a point system where children earn points for completing tasks, demonstrating positive behaviors, or reaching goals. These points can be redeemed for privileges or rewards, such as extra screen time or a special treat.

2. Tailor Rewards to Their Interests

Understanding your child's interests helps you choose rewards that resonate with them:

- **Discover What They Love**: Have a conversation about what rewards would be meaningful for them. It could be as simple as choosing dinner for the week or a day off from chores.

- **Involve Kids in the Process**: Allow your child to contribute ideas for both tasks and corresponding rewards. When they have say in the process, they are more likely to feel invested.

Promoting Accountability

Having a system of accountability is just as important as providing incentives. It helps children understand that their actions—good or bad—have consequences, teaching them to take ownership of their responsibilities.

1. Set Clear Expectations

Clear expectations set the foundation for accountability:

- **Work Together**: Sit down with your child and discuss what responsibilities they have. Outline specific tasks and make sure they understand the expectations involved.

- **Use Visual Reminders**: Whether it's a family calendar or a chore chart, visual reminders help reinforce accountability by keeping the expectations front and center.

2. Regular Check-Ins

Regular check-ins play an essential role in promoting accountability and creating an open environment for discussion.

- **Schedule Weekly Meetings**: Dedicate specific times to discuss progress, accomplishments, and any areas for improvement. This ongoing communication allows for adjustments and reflections.

- **Encourage Self-Reflection**: After tasks are completed, ask questions like, "How did you feel about completing your chores?" or "What was difficult about studying for that test?" This practice encourages them to evaluate their performance and take ownership.

Teaching Consequences

1. **Natural Consequences**: Allow your child to experience the natural consequences of their actions. If they neglect to do homework, they may face lower grades. However, do this in a supportive manner, ready to help them understand and learn from the experience.

2. **Logical Consequences**: If homework isn't completed, a logical consequence might be a temporary loss of privileges, such as limited screen time. Make sure the consequence is related to the behavior in question.

   - **Be Consistent**: Consistency is key to effective consequences. When children know what to expect after failing to meet responsibilities, they are more likely to take those responsibilities seriously.

Encouraging Self-Discipline

Teaching self-discipline is like training a muscle. It requires consistent practice and reinforcement.

1. Gradual Increase of Responsibilities

Start with simple tasks and gradually increase their complexity. This method promotes self-discipline and builds confidence.

- **Start Small**: Assign manageable daily tasks, such as sorting laundry or completing one homework assignment. As they succeed, increase the responsibility.

- **Celebrate Progress**: Recognize achievements, no matter how small. Celebrations reinforce the idea that discipline leads to positive outcomes.

2. Offer Choices and Freedom

Autonomy encourages children to develop self-discipline naturally:

- **Encourage Decision-Making**: Give them choices related to their responsibilities, such as selecting which chores they want to complete first or how they will organize their homework. Encouraging decision-making fosters ownership and accountability.

- **Self-Monitoring**: Equip them with tools to self-monitor, such as planners or checklists. Teaching children to track their own responsibilities promotes self-management.

Building a Growth Mindset

Promoting a growth mindset helps children understand that persistence leads to improvement; it's about recognizing progress over perfection.

1. **Normalize Challenges**: Teach your child that challenges are part of the learning process. Engage them in conversation when they encounter a hurdle and affirm that their effort in overcoming difficulties is valuable.

2. **Praise Efforts, Not Just Results**: While it's essential to acknowledge accomplishments, emphasizing the importance of effort helps build resilience and encourages continued striving for improvement.

Conclusion of Chapter 6

Establishing an effective incentive system and promoting accountability can empower children to take ownership of their actions and responsibilities. By implementing structured incentives and teaching self-discipline, you help your child navigate their responsibilities on their own. In the next chapter, we'll discuss the art of negotiation—turning conflicts into constructive conversations and how to transform "no" into "yes" in a supportive, respectful manner.

Chapter 7: The Art of Negotiation - Turning 'No' into 'Yes'

The Art of Negotiation: Turning 'No' into 'Yes' with Your Kids

Negotiation isn't just some fancy term for haggling over prices at a flea market; it's a life skill that influences our everyday interactions. It's essential for effective communication, resolving conflicts, and—let's be honest—building mutual understanding. As parents, mastering the art of negotiation with your children can flip those daily challenges on their heads, transforming them into golden opportunities for teamwork and cooperation. Ready to dive in? Let's explore some effective negotiation strategies to turn those stubborn "no's" into enthusiastic "yes's"!

Understanding the Concept of Negotiation

So, what's the scoop on negotiation? At its heart, negotiation isn't about winning or bending anyone to your will. Instead, it's about finding that sweet spot where everyone feels heard and valued. This paves the way for collaboration. When you negotiate with your child, you're fostering a healthy dialogue that allows both of you to express your needs constructively. It's a total game-changer for parenting! Equipped with the right skills, you can ease those pesky power struggles, boost mutual respect, and empower your little ones to feel like they have a voice in their lives.

Why Kids Resist: Getting to the Heart of the "No"

Before we jump into the nitty-gritty of negotiation tactics, let's pause and unpack why kids sometimes dig their heels in and resist what you're asking. Understanding the whys behind their "no" can significantly enhance your approach. Here are a few familiar culprits:

1. **Desire for Independence**: As kids grow, they develop a fierce craving for independence. They want to navigate their own ship, making choices that feel right for them. When they say "no," it's often a way of grasping for that control.

2. **Emotional States**: We've all been there—after a long day at school, the last thing kids want to do is another task! When their emotions run high, they might push back simply because they feel overwhelmed.

3. **Fear of Failure**: Sometimes, a flat-out refusal masks deeper insecurities. Your child might resist because they're scared that they can't actually tackle what's being asked of them.

By tuning into these underlying factors, you can navigate negotiations with a lot more finesse—turning potential conflicts into opportunities for connection.

Essential Strategies for Effective Negotiation with Kids

Ready to transform those "no's" into "yes's"? Let's break down some enjoyable negotiation strategies that can make your encounters with your kids feel less like tense standoffs and more like empowering exchanges.

1. Build Rapport and Trust

Without trust, negotiations are like trying to navigate with a broken compass. If your child feels comfortable and connected to you, they're far more likely to engage meaningfully in dialogue.

- **Engage in Play**: Make time for games and activities your child loves. These moments build closeness and make tough conversations easier later on.

- **Use Humor**: Laughter can be your secret weapon. A dash of humor can lighten the mood, creating a relaxed atmosphere for negotiation.

2. Use Active Listening

Kids want to feel valued; showing that you care makes a world of difference.

- **Repeat and Reflect**: When your child says "no," try repeating back what you heard. For instance, "I hear that you don't want to do your homework right now because you're tired. Can we explore that?" This shows empathy and opens the door for more dialogue.

- **Ask Questions**: Flip the script and let them voice their views. Questions like "What makes you want to avoid cleaning your room?" can prompt them to share their thoughts and feelings.

3. Offer Choices

Instead of issuing commands like a general in battle, give your child options instead. Choices shift the power dynamic and give them more control.

- **Present Limited Options**: Offer a couple of choices that lead to the same desired outcome. Rather than saying, "You need to clean your room now," try,

"Would you like to clean your room first or tackle your homework?"

- **Incorporate Their Interests**: If they're resistant, let them suggest how to approach the task. Maybe say, "How would you like to start organizing your toys— by color or size?" This inclusion fosters a sense of participation.

4. Identify and Offer Incentives

Let's be real; kids love rewards! A little incentive can make them much more open to agreeing.

- **Explore Potential Rewards**: Talk about what they might find tempting for completing a task. Ask something like, "If you finish your homework, we can watch your favorite show together afterward."

- **Connect Tasks to Interests**: Link chores to fun activities afterward. If they help clean, promise them some extra game time in the evening. It'll be much easier to score a "yes!" when there's something to look forward to.

5. Highlight the Benefits

Help your kids see the reasoning behind your requests. When they understand the value of cooperation, they might be more inclined to jump on board.

- **Connect Tasks to Real-Life Benefits**: Explain how cleaning their room can clear space for fun activities. Or let them know that finishing homework now leads to better grades and more playtime later on.

- **Use "If, Then" Statements**: Create clear cause-and-effect scenarios. For example, "If you finish your chores now, then we can have pizza for dinner." It's straightforward and effective!

6. Involve Them in Rule-Making

Want to boost compliance? Empower your children by inviting them to help set family rules and expectations.

- **Family Meetings**: Host regular family discussions about rules and responsibilities. When kids have a say, they're much more likely to follow the guidelines.

- **Collaborate on Solutions**: If there's a struggle with a task, invite them into the problem-solving conversation. Say something like, "What would help you complete your homework each day?" This encourages ownership and develops their problem-solving skills.

Managing Disagreements During Negotiation

Even with all your best strategies, disagreements can still arise. Having techniques for conflict management can keep discussions productive.

- **Stay Calm and Composed**: When things get heated, take a deep breath. Your calm demeanor sets the tone for the interaction.

- **Be Open to Compromise**: Finding a middle ground is crucial. If your child resists, try saying, "How about we try this for a week, and then we can see how it works for both of us?"

- **Know When to Walk Away**: Sometimes, stepping back is the best option. If emotions are running high, suggest a break. Let your child know it's perfectly fine to cool off before revisiting the conversation.

Conclusion of Chapter 7

Negotiation isn't just a skill; it's a vital tool that can unlock cooperation and understanding between you and your kids. By practicing active listening, offering choices, involving them in rule-making, and highlighting benefits, you can turn frustrating moments of resistance into engaging, productive conversations.

In the next chapter, we'll delve into the essential topic of emotional regulation—teaching children how to manage their emotions effectively. With these skills in hand, you'll pave the way for even more fruitful interactions. Here's to transforming challenges into exciting opportunities!

Chapter 8: Emotional Regulation - Teaching Kids to Manage Frustration

Emotional regulation is the ability to manage and respond to one's emotions in a healthy and constructive way. For children, learning this vital skill is crucial as it lays the foundation for successful interactions, effective communication, and overall well-being. This chapter will explore techniques and strategies for teaching kids how to manage their frustrations and emotions effectively, leading to improved behavior and a more harmonious family environment.

Understanding Emotional Regulation

Before we can teach our children about emotional regulation, it's essential to understand what it means. Emotional regulation involves recognizing one's emotional state, understanding its effects, and implementing strategies to respond appropriately. Here are some fundamental aspects of emotional regulation:

1. **Emotional Awareness**: Recognizing and identifying one's emotions is the first step in managing them. Children must learn to differentiate between feelings such as anger, sadness, frustration, and excitement.
2. **Understanding Triggers**: Identifying what events or situations trigger specific emotions can help children anticipate their responses and prepare for them.
3. **Implementing Coping Strategies**: Children need tools and techniques to manage their emotions constructively without resorting to negative behaviors such as defiance or withdrawal.

The Importance of Emotional Regulation for Children

Investing in emotional regulation skills yields significant benefits, including:

- **Improved Relationships**: Children who can manage their emotions effectively are more likely to develop healthy relationships with peers, adults, and family members.
- **Better Academic Performance**: Emotional regulation contributes to better focus, perseverance, and problem-solving skills, leading to improved academic performance.
- **Reduced Behavioral Issues**: Teaching emotional regulation can decrease instances of defiance, tantrums, and other disruptive behaviors commonly associated with frustration.

Strategies for Teaching Emotional Regulation

1. Model Emotional Regulation

Children learn a great deal from observing their parents and caregivers. Modeling healthy emotional regulation sets an example they can emulate.

- **Share Your Emotions**: When you experience a difficult emotional situation, verbalize your feelings and how you cope. For example, you might say, "I feel frustrated because I have a lot to do. I'm going to take a deep breath and step outside for a moment to collect my thoughts."
- **Demonstrate Coping Techniques**: Show your child the techniques you use to manage stress or frustration, whether it's taking deep breaths, counting to ten, or going for a walk.

2. Teach Identifying Emotions

Help your children label their feelings by using clear, age-appropriate language.

- **Emotion Charts**: Create an emotion chart with various facial expressions representing different feelings. Encourage your child to identify how they're feeling, making it easier for them to recognize emotions in themselves and others.
- **Discuss Feelings**: Incorporate discussions about emotions into daily conversations. After watching a movie or reading a book, ask questions like, "How do you think the character felt in that situation? How would you feel?"

3. Encourage Open Dialogue about Feelings

Create a safe space for your child to express their feelings without fear of judgment.

- **Active Listening**: When your child shares their feelings, listen attentively. Validate their emotions by saying, "I understand that you feel upset; it's okay to feel that way."
- **Ask Open-Ended Questions**: Encourage deeper discussions about feelings by asking questions like, "What made you feel that way?" or "What do you think you can do when you feel frustrated?"

4. Provide Coping Strategies

Teach practical coping strategies that they can use when feeling overwhelmed or frustrated.

- **Deep Breathing Techniques**: Introduce deep breathing exercises, like inhaling for four counts, holding for four counts, and exhaling for four counts. Practice together when your child is calm so they can recall the technique when emotions run high.

- **Counting to Ten**: Encourage your child to pause and count to ten before reacting when they feel intense emotions. This can help them create some distance from the moment and think through their response.
- **Mindfulness Practices**: Introduce simple mindfulness exercises, like focusing on sensory experiences (tuning into what they can see, hear, feel). This practice can help ground them when emotions are intense.

5. Role-Playing Scenarios

Role-playing can help children practice emotional regulation in real-life situations.

- **Practice Coping Techniques in Context**: Create scenarios where your child might feel frustrated—for example, losing a game or encountering a challenging homework problem. Have them role-play a positive response to the situation.
- **Use Puppets or Toys**: If your child finds it challenging to role-play directly, using puppets or toys can make the exercise fun and approachable.

Teaching Problem-Solving Skills

Problem-solving skills are essential for emotional regulation. Teaching children to approach challenges with a solution-oriented mindset helps them feel more equipped to handle frustration.

1. **Identify the Problem**: Encourage your child to articulate the problem causing their frustration. For example, "What's bothering you right now? Can you describe what's happening?"
2. **Brainstorm Solutions**: Once the problem is clear, ask your child to think of potential solutions. Encourage them to come up with multiple options and consider the pros and cons of each.

3. **Choose a Solution Together**: After discussing possible solutions, help them select one to try. By involving children in this process, they learn to take responsibility for their emotions and reactions.

Reinforcing Emotional Regulation

Reinforcement is vital for solidifying emotional regulation practices.

- **Praise Efforts**: Acknowledge when your child uses emotional regulation techniques successfully. Positive reinforcement when they handle frustrations well can encourage them to continue those behaviors.
- **Create an Emotion Journal**: Encourage your child to keep an emotion journal where they can write about their feelings and the strategies they used to cope. This exercise can enhance self-awareness and reinforce learning.

Conclusion of Chapter 8

Teaching emotional regulation equips children with tools to navigate their feelings and interactions positively. As children learn to identify their emotions, communicate openly, and implement coping strategies, they develop the skills necessary to manage frustration and engage in healthy, productive behavior. In the next chapter, we will delve into encouraging independence—fostering a sense of responsibility that empowers children to take ownership of their actions and decisions.

Chapter 9: Encouraging Independence - Fostering a Sense of Responsibility

Encouraging independence in children is a crucial aspect of their development. When children learn to take responsibility for their actions and make decisions, they build self-confidence, problem-solving skills, and resilience. In this chapter, we will explore effective strategies for fostering independence and instilling a sense of responsibility in your children, empowering them to thrive in their daily lives.

Understanding the Importance of Independence

Independence is about more than just letting kids do things on their own; it's about fostering an internal sense of control and competence. Here's why encouraging independence matters:

1. **Building Self-Confidence**: When children successfully manage tasks independently, their self-esteem grows. This sense of accomplishment reinforces the belief that they can tackle challenges on their own.
2. **Encouraging Decision-Making Skills**: Independence allows children to practice making decisions and understanding the consequences of their choices. These skills are essential for navigating everyday challenges and life decisions.
3. **Promoting Resilience**: Learning to face setbacks and challenges independently equips children with the skills to bounce back from difficulties. They become more adaptive and resourceful.

4. **Fostering a Sense of Responsibility**: Independence comes with accountability. Children learn that their actions have consequences, helping them develop a sense of responsibility for their behavior and interactions.

Strategies to Foster Independence

Encouraging independence in children involves gradual steps that allow them to build confidence and skills. Here are effective strategies to promote independence and responsibility:

1. Start Early

Introducing independence at a young age lays the foundation for future growth. Children are naturally curious and eager to explore, so seize these moments to promote independence.

- **Age-Appropriate Chores**: Assign simple, age-appropriate chores to very young children. Tasks like putting away toys, helping with meal preparation, or sorting laundry enable them to take on responsibilities.
- **Encourage Exploration**: Allow young children to navigate new environments with supervision. Whether it's a local park or a new playdate, encourage them to interact with peers and explore their surroundings independently.

2. Give Choices

Offering choices is a powerful way to encourage independence. It allows children to feel a sense of control over their decisions.

- **Options for Routine Tasks**: For daily activities, provide choices that lead to the same outcome. For example, "Would you like to wear the blue shirt or the red one today?" or "Do you want to do your homework now or after dinner?"
- **Encourage Meal Selection**: When planning meals, involve your child by allowing them to choose from a range of healthy options. This practice empowers them to make decisions about their eating habits.

3. Teach Problem-Solving Skills

Problem-solving is an essential aspect of independence. Teaching children to think critically about challenges fosters self-reliance.

- **Encourage Exploration**: When your child faces a problem, ask guiding questions to prompt their thinking. For instance, instead of providing an immediate solution, ask, "What do you think you could try?"
- **Give Them Space to Experiment**: Allow your child to solve problems on their own. Resist the urge to jump in and offer solutions. If they are struggling with a task, observe quietly and step in only if necessary.

4. Support Goal Setting

Goal setting helps children take ownership of their actions and aspirations. It encourages them to visualize their progress and take accountability for their efforts.

- **Short-Term and Long-Term Goals**: Help your child establish both short-term (daily or weekly) and long-term (monthly or yearly) goals. For younger children, keep goals simple and concrete. As they grow, goals can become more ambitious.

- **Create a Visual Tracker**: Use a chart or poster where they can visually track their progress. Celebrating milestones along the way reinforces the significance of their efforts.

5. Encourage Self-Care

Teaching children self-care skills is a vital step in fostering independence. Understanding how to manage personal needs instills confidence.

- **Daily Routines**: Guide your child in establishing routines for personal care tasks, from brushing teeth to dressing themselves. Encourage them to complete these tasks independently.
- **Teach Organization**: Help your child understand the importance of organization. Use tools like planners, checklists, or labeled storage bins to help them manage their belongings and responsibilities effectively.
-

6. Provide Opportunities for Participation

Involving children in family decisions and tasks enhances their sense of belonging and independence.

- **Family Meetings**: Hold regular family meetings to discuss plans, schedules, and responsibilities. Involve your child in the decision-making process to promote ownership.
- **Team Projects**: Include them in family projects—whether it's gardening, redecorating a room, or planning a trip. When children see their contributions matter, it boosts their sense of autonomy.

7. Accept Mistakes as Learning Opportunities

Learning from mistakes is an integral part of developing independence. Allowing children to make mistakes teaches them resilience and accountability.

- **Normalize Failure**: Discuss the inevitability of making mistakes. Help them understand that mistakes are valuable learning experiences and that everyone encounters challenges.
- **Guide Reflection**: If your child makes a mistake or faces a setback, guide them in reflecting on what happened. Ask questions like, "What would you do differently next time?" or "What did you learn from this situation?"

The Role of Encouragement and Positive Reinforcement

Encouragement is vital in reinforcing independent behavior.

1. **Praise Efforts, Not Just Outcomes**: Celebrate your child's efforts and initiatives, regardless of the outcome. Phrases like "I'm proud of how hard you tried" help cultivate a growth mindset.
2. **Use Positive Reinforcement**: Strategies such as sticker charts or reward systems can motivate children to take on responsibilities. When they complete tasks independently, recognize their achievements with praise or tangible rewards.

Supporting Independence Through Patience

Fostering independence takes time and requires patience. Here's how to navigate this journey thoughtfully:

- **Be Patient and Understanding**: Recognize that your child may struggle with new tasks at first. Offer encouragement and avoid expressing frustration. Remind them that practice leads to improvement.
- **Celebrate Small Wins**: Acknowledge progress, no matter how small. This celebration reinforces positive behavior and motivates continued efforts.

Conclusion of Chapter 9

Encouraging independence fosters a sense of responsibility in children, empowering them to take ownership of their actions and decisions. By providing opportunities for choice, instilling problem-solving skills, and supporting goal-setting, you help equip your child with the tools necessary for personal growth and development. In the next chapter, we will explore the importance of routine and structure—the backbone of productivity that helps children thrive in their daily lives.

Chapter 10: Routine and Structure - The Backbone of Productivity

Crafting Routines: The Backbone of Child Development

Establishing routines and structure is key to helping children successfully navigate their daily lives. Routines offer predictability, reinforce desirable habits, and create a comforting sense of security within the family. In this chapter, we'll explore why routines are so important, the myriad benefits they bring to your child, and practical strategies for implementing effective routines that boost both productivity and overall well-being.

Understanding Routines and Structure

What Exactly Are Routines?

Routines are essentially sequences of actions or behaviors that are repeated regularly, sort of like a well-rehearsed dance. They can range from straightforward, daily tasks to more structured weekly schedules. Creating routines involves not just establishing a handy checklist but ensuring those tasks fit into an organized framework that promotes emotional comfort and allows your child to manage their time efficiently.

The Importance of Routines

So why are routines so essential? Let's break it down:

- **Predictability**: Children thrive on knowing what to expect. Routines help reduce anxiety by laying down a consistent path for them to follow. When they have a structured day, they feel more secure and at ease.

- **Skill Development**: Routines aren't just tasks; they're opportunities! Through routine, kids develop vital life skills like time management, organization, and an all-important sense of responsibility. As they learn to navigate these routines, they gain autonomy and confidence.

- **Behavioral Regulation**: A well-structured environment minimizes chaos and lessens the chances of conflict. When kids know what's expected of them, they're far less likely to resist or act out. It's like giving them a map to navigate their day!

- **Time Management**: Routines teach children how to allocate their time effectively. They show kids how to prioritize responsibilities while still leaving space for fun and relaxation—without feeling overwhelmed.

Creating Effective Routines

Crafting routines that resonate with your family isn't a one-size-fits-all approach; it requires intention, flexibility, and a splash of consistency. Here's how to get started:

1. Identify Key Areas for Routine Development

First off, pinpoint where a structured routine could work wonders in your child's life. Here are some common areas that might benefit:

- **Morning Routine**: A well-structured morning can set a positive tone for the day. Think about everything from waking up to getting dressed, eating breakfast, and preparing for school.

- **Homework Routine**: Designating a specific time and space for homework can greatly improve focus and efficiency. It's all about creating a conducive learning environment.

- **Evening Routine**: A consistent bedtime routine is essential for promoting relaxation and ensuring your little ones get the rest they need to thrive.

2. Involve Your Child

Want to boost compliance? Get your child involved in creating these routines! This nurtures ownership and teaches essential decision-making skills.

- **Collaborate on Routines**: Sit down together and sketch out a typical day. Ask your child how they envision their mornings or evenings. This approach not only validates their opinions but also helps them feel invested in the routines you create.

- **Visual Schedule**: Why not craft a colorful visual schedule? Use pictures or charts to illustrate the steps of each routine. This is especially beneficial for younger children who are still mastering reading skills!

3. Establish Clear Expectations

Clear expectations are crucial for successful routines. When children know what's required of them, it prevents confusion and resistance.

- **Break Down Tasks**: Outline each component of the routine step by step. For a morning routine, include everything from getting out of bed to brushing teeth and packing their backpack. It's all about clarity!

- **Set Time Limits**: Assign approximate time limits to each task. This practice helps children grasp how long different activities should take, promoting better time management.

4. Practice Consistency

Consistency is the glue that holds routines together. The more regular and predictable they become, the more likely kids are to stick to them.

- **Daily Reinforcement**: Keep the same structure every day, even on weekends. This familiarity helps children internalize routines over time.

- **Adjust as Needed**: Life is dynamic, so remain flexible. If changes occur—say, extracurricular activities or family events—discuss how these fit into the established routines. Adaptability is a valuable life lesson!

5. Use Positive Reinforcement

Celebrating your child's efforts to follow routines can go a long way in reinforcing positive behavior.

- **Praise Efforts**: Be vocal about your pride! Acknowledge when your child sticks to the routine. Simple phrases like, "I'm so proud of how well you handled your morning routine today!" can work wonders.

- **Reward Systems**: Introduce a little incentive! Implement a rewards system—be it stickers, points, or small treats—to motivate them to adhere to routines.

Maintaining Flexibility Within Structure

While routines are critical, don't forget that flexibility is equally important. Life is full of surprises, and children must learn to adapt to unexpected changes.

- **Encourage Adaptability**: Talk with your child about the importance of adjusting when plans change. Use phrases like, "Sometimes things don't go as planned, and that's okay. Let's brainstorm how we can adjust together."

- **Practice Scenario Planning**: Role-playing can be fun! Walk through how to handle disruptions. For instance, if homework isn't finished due to a late night, discuss how your child can adjust their schedule the next day.

The Role of Routines in Emotional Well-Being

Routines do more than streamline tasks; they significantly contribute to emotional well-being by providing children with a sense of stability. Consider these key emotional benefits:

- **Reduced Anxiety**: Predictability lowers anxiety. Kids who know what's coming each day feel more grounded and less frightened by the unknown.

- **Increased Confidence**: Successfully tackling daily routines builds self-esteem. Children who navigate their responsibilities feel capable and competent.

- **Enhanced Bonding**: Routines aren't just about tasks —they foster connections. Shared routines, particularly during family time like dinner or bedtime, strengthen familial bonds and create cherished memories.

Conclusion of Chapter 10

In conclusion, establishing routines and structure is essential for enhancing children's productivity, emotional well-being, and overall functioning. By involving your kids in the creation of routines, clarifying expectations, and employing positive reinforcement, you lay the groundwork for a productive and enjoyable environment.

In the next chapter, we will explore the power of positive reinforcement—how celebrating small victories can motivate children and reinforce desirable behaviors, cultivating a nurturing atmosphere for growth and learning. Let's embark on this journey together!

Chapter 11: Positive Reinforcement - Celebrating Small Victories

Positive reinforcement is a powerful tool in parenting that encourages desired behaviors and promotes motivation. By celebrating accomplishments—no matter how small—you can foster a positive environment that reinforces good behavior, bolsters self-esteem, and helps children develop a growth mindset. In this chapter, we will explore the concept of positive reinforcement, its psychological underpinnings, and practical strategies for effectively implementing it in your parenting approach.

Understanding Positive Reinforcement
What is Positive Reinforcement?
Positive reinforcement involves providing a reward or positive stimulus after a desired behavior is exhibited, making it more likely that the behavior will occur again in the future. This technique is based on the principles of operant conditioning, which suggests that behaviors followed by positive outcomes are encouraged, while those followed by negative outcomes tend to be discouraged.

Why It Works:

1. **Increases Motivation**: Children are more likely to engage in tasks when they anticipate positive feedback or rewards following their efforts.
2. **Builds Self-Esteem**: Recognizing children's achievements reinforces their belief in their capabilities and promotes a sense of accomplishment.

3. **Enhances Positive Behavior**: Positive reinforcement not only encourages desired actions but can also reduce unwanted behaviors by shifting focus to what is being done correctly.

Strategies for Effective Positive Reinforcement

1. Be Specific with Praise

When you provide positive reinforcement, specificity matters. Vague compliments can sometimes lead to confusion about what behavior is being reinforced.

- **Be Descriptive**: Instead of saying, "Good job," use specific language that clarifies what they did well. For example, "I love how you put away your toys without being asked. That shows responsibility!"
- **Focus on Effort Over Outcome**: Encouraging effort over success fosters a growth mindset. Compliment them on their hard work with statements like, "You studied really hard for that test, and I'm proud of your dedication."

2. Use Timely Reinforcement

The timing of your reinforcement is crucial in building connections between behavior and feedback.

- **Immediate Feedback**: Reinforce immediately after the desired behavior occurs. For instance, if your child completes their chores without prompting, provide praise right away to solidify the connection.
- **Regular Check-Ins**: During routines, check in with your child and provide affirmative feedback. Acknowledge positive actions in the moment, which helps keep motivation high.

3. Implement Reward Systems

Establishing a reward system can create motivation for continued positive behavior. Here's how to set one up effectively:

- **Choose Appropriate Rewards**: Identify rewards that are meaningful to your child. This could range from extra playtime, screen time, or a small treat. Get their input to ensure the rewards resonate with them.
- **Create a Chart**: Use a visual chart or sticker system to track progress. For every task completed or positive behavior exhibited, they can earn a sticker or point. Once enough are collected, they can redeem them for a reward.

4. Celebrate Achievements

Celebration serves as a powerful form of reinforcement. It not only acknowledges effort but also builds a culture of appreciation within the family.

- **Create Celebratory Rituals**: Establish rituals for acknowledging achievements. For example, after completing a big project, celebrate with a family movie night or a homemade dessert party.
- **Encourage Self-Celebration**: Teach children to acknowledge and celebrate their victories. For instance, they could write down their accomplishments each week in a journal, boosting their self-awareness and pride.

5. Foster a Positive Environment

Creating a positive and encouraging atmosphere is essential for effective positive reinforcement.

- **Model Positive Behaviors**: Demonstrate positivity and encouragement in your interactions with others. Children learn by observing, and seeing you celebrate success in others teaches them to embrace positivity.
- **Limit Negative Feedback**: While constructive criticism is necessary, try to balance it with encouragement. Rather than focusing solely on what needs improvement, frame challenges positively. For example, "I noticed you struggled with that homework. Let's work together to make it easier next time!"

Utilizing Positive Reinforcement in Everyday Life

1. **In Daily Routines**: Incorporate reinforcement into daily tasks such as chores or homework. Praise children for completing their responsibilities and helping others around the house.
2. **During Learning Activities**: Acknowledge effort during learning experiences, whether it is in homework, reading, or creative projects. Reinforce the idea that hard work pays off.
3. **Encourage Teamwork**: If your child is part of a team or group activity, celebrate their contributions to the team's success. Acknowledge how their collaboration and support helped achieve a common goal.

Avoiding Over-Reliance on Rewards

While positive reinforcement is effective, it's important to avoid over-reliance on tangible rewards. Here are some strategies to help balance this relationship:

- **Gradually Shift Focus**: Begin with tangible rewards, but gradually shift to more intrinsic motivations as children internalize the behaviors. For example, as they become more responsible, praise them for their maturity rather than focusing solely on rewards.
- **Encourage Self-Motivation**: Teach children to identify and celebrate their internal motivations. Discuss how completing tasks makes them feel and emphasize the sense of accomplishment that accompanies achievement.

Conclusion of Chapter 11

Positive reinforcement is a powerful parenting tool that encourages desired behavior and motivates children to strive for success. By being specific with praise, offering timely reinforcement, and celebrating victories, you create an environment that promotes growth, resilience, and self-esteem. In the next chapter, we will explore mindfulness and relaxation techniques—effective practices that can help improve focus and emotional well-being in children.

Chapter 12: Mindfulness and Relaxation Techniques for Focus

In today's fast-paced world, children face a myriad of distractions and pressures that can lead to heightened stress, anxiety, and difficulty focusing. Mindfulness and relaxation techniques serve as valuable tools to help children manage their emotions, enhance their concentration, and improve overall well-being. This chapter will explore the principles of mindfulness, various relaxation techniques, and how to incorporate these practices into your child's daily routine.

Understanding Mindfulness
What is Mindfulness?
Mindfulness is the practice of paying attention to the present moment without judgment. It involves being aware of one's thoughts, feelings, and bodily sensations while cultivating an attitude of acceptance. By teaching children to be mindful, we empower them to better manage their thoughts and emotions, leading to improved focus and emotional regulation.

Benefits of Mindfulness for Children
1. **Enhanced Focus and Concentration**: Mindfulness helps improve attention span and concentration, making it easier for children to engage in tasks such as homework or chores.
2. **Reduced Stress and Anxiety**: Engaging in mindfulness practices promotes relaxation, helping children manage stress and anxiety that may arise from school pressures or social interactions.

3. **Improved Emotional Regulation**: Mindful practices teach children to recognize their emotions, fostering a greater understanding of how to respond to challenging situations calmly and effectively.
4. **Better Social Skills**: Mindfulness can enhance empathy and connection with others, leading to improved social interactions and relationships.

Mindfulness Techniques for Children

1. Deep Breathing Exercises

Deep breathing is a simple yet effective mindfulness technique that can help children calm themselves and refocus.

- **Belly Breathing**: Teach your child to place a hand on their belly and take slow, deep breaths, feeling their belly rise and fall. As they inhale for a count of four, hold for four, and exhale for four, encourage them to visualize stress leaving their body with each breath.
- **Breathing Buddies**: Use a small stuffed animal or pillow, allowing children to place it on their belly. As they breathe deeply, they watch the "buddy" rise and fall with each breath.

2. Mindful Observation

Encourage your child to engage their senses by observing their surroundings mindfully.

- **Nature Walks**: Take a walk outdoors and focus on the sights, sounds, and smells around you. Ask your child to describe what they see: "What colors are the leaves? What sounds can you hear?" This practice can be calming and enhance their appreciation for nature.

- **Mindful Eating**: Practice mindfulness during snack or meal times. Have your child take small bites, savoring each flavor and texture. Encourage them to notice the colors and smells of their food, making mealtimes a more enjoyable experience.

3. Guided Imagery

Guided imagery is a relaxation technique that involves visualizing peaceful and calming scenes.

- **Create a Calming Visualization**: Help your child create a mental picture of a calming scene—such as a beach, forest, or any place that makes them feel happy and relaxed. Encourage them to close their eyes, take deep breaths, and visualize themselves in that place.
- **Storytelling Practice**: Lead them through a calming story where they picture themselves on an adventure in a peaceful setting. Use descriptive language to immerse them in the experience.

4. Body Scan Meditation

Body scan meditation encourages children to notice physical sensations in different parts of their body, promoting relaxation and awareness.

- **Guided Practice**: Lead your child in a body scan by asking them to lie down comfortably and focus on each part of their body, starting from their toes and moving upwards. Encourage them to observe any tension, inviting them to relax each part as they focus on it.
- **Tune into Sensations**: Encourage them to notice how their body feels, acknowledging sensations like tightness or warmth, and consciously relaxing those areas.

Incorporating Mindfulness into Daily Routines

1. **Mindfulness Moments**: Dedicate a few minutes daily to mindfulness practices, whether it's during breakfast, before school, or at bedtime. Establishing regular mindfulness moments helps create consistency.
2. **Check-Ins**: During family gatherings or even meals, take a moment to check in with everyone's emotional state. Ask open-ended questions like, "How are you feeling today?" This dialogue encourages mindfulness and emotional awareness.
3. **Mindful Transitions**: Use mindfulness exercises during transitions, such as before entering a new environment (like school) or after a busy day. Encourage children to take a few deep breaths before moving on to the next activity.
4. **Mindfulness Reminders**: Use visual reminders, such as sticky notes around the house, to prompt mindfulness throughout the day. These can serve as cues to take a deep breath, observe surroundings, or practice gratitude.

Teaching Relaxation Techniques

In addition to mindfulness, relaxation techniques help alleviate stress and improve focus. Here are some effective relaxation strategies:

1. Progressive Muscle Relaxation

This technique involves tensing and relaxing different muscle groups, promoting physical relaxation.

- **Guided Sessions**: Lead your child through a series of muscle tensing and relaxing exercises. Start with their toes, encouraging them to tense the muscles for a few seconds and then release, working their way up to the head.

- **Visualization**: Combine this with visualization by asking them to imagine releasing tension with each exhale.

2. Yoga for Kids

Yoga can be an excellent way for children to develop mindfulness and relaxation skills while also promoting physical health.

- **Kid-Friendly Classes**: Explore kid-friendly yoga classes or online resources that offer playful poses and engaging themes. Encourage them to participate regularly as a family activity.
- **Yoga as a Calm-Down Strategy**: Use yoga exercises when your child feels overwhelmed or anxious. Simple poses like Child's Pose or Downward Dog can help them regain composure.

3. Journaling

Encouraging children to express their thoughts and feelings through writing can promote reflection and relaxation.

- **Daily Gratitude Journals**: Help your child keep a gratitude journal where they can jot down things they are thankful for each day. This practice shifts focus from stressors to positive aspects of life.
- **Expressive Writing**: Encourage them to write about their feelings, whether happy or sad. This exercise allows them to process emotions and gain clarity.

Conclusion of Chapter 12

Mindfulness and relaxation techniques are powerful tools that equip children with the skills needed to manage stress, enhance focus, and improve emotional regulation. By integrating these practices into daily routines, you empower your child to navigate life's challenges more effectively. In the next chapter, we will explore engaging activities to make work fun—turning chores and responsibilities into enjoyable experiences, fostering a more positive attitude toward tasks.

Chapter 13: Engaging Activities to Make Work Fun

Turning Chores into Fun: A Playful Approach to Responsibilities

Transforming responsibilities and chores into engaging activities is a supercharged strategy for motivating children to jump in with enthusiasm—yes, you heard that right! By adopting a playful approach and sprinkling enjoyable elements into daily tasks, your little ones can learn to connect work with fun instead of mere obligation. This chapter will explore creative techniques and activities designed to make work appealing, fostering a positive attitude toward responsibilities.

The Importance of Making Work Fun

Why bother making chores enjoyable? Well, consider these benefits:

- **Increased Motivation**: When kids view tasks as enjoyable rather than burdensome, they're much more likely to get involved willingly and complete them without the usual nagging.

- **Enhanced Learning**: Fun activities reinforce learning through play, allowing children to grasp concepts better and apply them with ease. Learning doesn't have to be dull!

- **Development of Positive Habits**: Associating responsibilities with fun helps cultivate lifelong positive habits. When they enjoy chores or studying, they're more likely to carry those behaviors into adulthood.

- **Strengthened Family Bonds**: Fun activities promote family participation, making chores a collaborative effort that solidifies relationships and creates lasting memories.

Strategies to Make Work Fun

Ready to transform those daunting chores into exciting escapades? Here's how to make work feel like a celebration!

1. Gamify Responsibilities

Who says chores have to be boring? Turn them into thrilling games that spark excitement!

- **Chore Challenges**: Get the competitive spirit flowing! Set challenges to see who can complete their chores the fastest. For example, "Let's time how quickly you can tidy your room! Ready, set, go!"

- **Reward Points**: Introduce a point system for completed chores, where children earn points based on task difficulty or speed. Set fun milestones for rewards, such as a family movie night or letting them choose the next weekend activity.

- **Treasure Hunts**: Turn cleaning into an adventurous treasure hunt! Hide small rewards or clues around the house that lead to a bigger prize. Cleaning and decluttering? A treasure chest awaits at the end!

2. Use Music and Dance

Music can work wonders, transforming any task into a vibrant experience.

- **Create Playlists**: Craft chore-specific playlists filled with energizing songs. Play them during chores and encourage kids to dance and sing along as they work. Grooving while cleaning? Yes, please!

- **Dance Parties**: Incorporate mini dance breaks between tasks. After finishing a section of their chores, let them take a minute to shake it out and celebrate before diving back in.

3. Incorporate Themed Activities

Themes add excitement and creativity to otherwise mundane tasks.

- **Seasonal Themes**: Align chores with the seasons! For example, a "spring cleaning" can double as a gardening party, while winter chores might include festive decorating fun while tidying up.

- **Role Play**: Infuse role play into chores for an extra layer of excitement. Pretend you're restaurant staff while setting the table or cleaning, challenging them to be the best "chef" by organizing the kitchen.

Making Homework Engaging

Homework can often feel like a chore to kids, but several strategies can make learning engaging and fun:

1. Study Groups

Why not turn homework into a social event?

- **Joint Study Sessions**: Encourage your child to form study groups with friends for regular homework sessions. Collaborative learning can boost motivation and make studying enjoyable!

- **Homework Parties**: Host occasional "homework parties!" Serve snacks and schedule breaks to keep kids motivated and engaged in their assignments—because who doesn't love snacks?

2. Interactive Learning Tools

Utilize engaging resources tailored to your child's learning style.

- **Educational Apps and Games**: Introduce educational apps or online games that blend learning with play, reinforcing concepts from school while keeping things fun.

- **Hands-On Projects**: Whenever possible, incorporate hands-on projects related to homework or subject matter. Think science experiments or creative writing through storytelling—learning can be an adventure!

3. Thematic Study Days

Why not spice up learning with thematic study days focused on specific subjects?

- **Cultural Days**: Dedicate a day to explore a country or culture through food, crafts, and projects. This hands-on experience allows children to engage with learning in a dynamic way.

- **Superhero Study**: Transform learning into an incredible adventure, where your child becomes a "superhero" tackling various subjects. Use colorful visuals and exciting narratives to keep them hooked on different tasks.

Encouraging Teamwork and Collaboration

Why not make responsibilities a team effort? Collaborative tasks can teach kids how to work together while making the experience enjoyable.

- **Family Chores**: Assign family tasks where everyone participates simultaneously, such as cleaning the living room or cooking dinner. Turn chores into a team activity where each person has a role to play!

- **Create a Team Spirit**: Foster a collaborative atmosphere by setting collective goals. When your family accomplishes tasks together, celebrate those achievements as a unit—cheers all around!

Making Routine Tasks Enjoyable

Daily routines can sometimes feel repetitive. Here's how to inject some fun into those everyday tasks:

- **Color-Coding Lists**: Use colorful charts or lists that allow children to mark off tasks creatively. Incorporating vibrant colors can make completing chores feel more like a fun art project.

- **Themed Dress-Up Days**: Let creativity run wild by incorporating dress-up themes for specific tasks on certain days. Gardening becomes a "hat day," or cooking transforms into "chef hat day." Now that's a fun twist!

- **Positive Visuals**: Create a "Victory Wall" where completed chores or homework can be prominently displayed. This encourages children to take pride in their work, providing a visual representation of their accomplishments.

Wrapping Up Chapter 13

Making work enjoyable requires creativity and a willingness to transform daily tasks into engaging activities. By gamifying responsibilities, incorporating music, using themes, and celebrating collaborative efforts, you create a positive environment where tasks are met with enthusiasm —not resistance.

In the next chapter, we'll explore the importance of modeling behavior—how parents can lead by example to instill values, responsibility, and good habits in their children. Let's set the stage for growth and learning together!

Chapter 14: Modeling Behavior - Leading by Example

As parents and caregivers, our behavior profoundly influences the way children perceive the world and learn to navigate it. Children are keen observers; they emulate the actions, attitudes, and values exhibited by the adults around them. Modeling positive behavior is one of the most effective strategies for instilling good habits, responsibility, and emotional intelligence in children. In this chapter, we will explore the significance of modeling behavior and practical strategies for leading by example.

The Power of Modeling

Why Modeling Matters

1. **Influence on Behavior**: Children learn primarily through observation. They are likely to imitate the behaviors, expressions, and approaches of their parents. Positive modeling can promote the values and attitudes you wish to see in your child.
2. **Establishing Norms**: By modeling desired behaviors, you help establish family norms and standards. When children see parents engaged in specific behaviors, they learn what is expected of them and develop patterns that reflect those norms.
3. **Building Trust and Connection**: Demonstrating positive behaviors fosters trust and strengthens the parent-child relationship. When children witness authenticity in their parents, they are more likely to feel secure and connected.

4. **Promoting Emotional Regulation**: Children observe how their parents manage emotions and challenges. By modeling effective emotional regulation, parents can teach children how to respond to adversity and frustration constructively.

Strategies for Effective Modeling

1. Be Conscious of Your Actions

1. **Self-Awareness**: Reflect on your behaviors and how they might impact your child. Consider how you handle stress, communicate with others, and manage challenges. Your self-awareness sets the tone for how your child perceives these situations.
2. **Consistency**: Strive for consistency in your actions and words. If you emphasize the importance of kindness but display impatience or frustration, it sends mixed signals to your child.

2. Communicate Openly and Honestly

1. **Admissions of Error**: It's okay to admit mistakes in front of your child. Acknowledging that everyone makes errors teaches them resilience and encourages them to accept their own mistakes as learning opportunities.
2. **Practice Transparency**: When discussing your decisions or feelings, invite your child into the conversation. For instance, if you are feeling stressed about work, share your feelings openly and explain how you plan to cope productively.

3. Demonstrate Positive Coping Strategies

1. **Emotional Regulation**: Exhibit healthy ways of managing stress, frustration, and other emotions. When faced with a challenge, verbalize your coping strategies, such as taking deep breaths, going for a walk, or talking to a friend.
2. **Problem-Solving Skills**: Show how you approach challenges calmly and rationally. Share your thought process with your child as you tackle a problem, encouraging them to adopt similar strategies.

4. Engage in Positive Relationships

1. **Model Healthy Interactions**: Demonstrate respectful communication and conflict resolution in relationships with friends, family members, and coworkers. Highlight the importance of listening, being patient, and communicating effectively.
2. **Community Engagement**: Involve your child in community activities, such as volunteering or helping a neighbor. Modeling compassion and community service teaches them to value kindness and empathy.

Encouraging Responsibility through Example

To foster a sense of responsibility in your child, it's essential to model responsible behavior consistently.

1. Demonstrate Task Management

1. **Daily Routines**: Effectively manage your own daily routines. When children witness you efficiently completing tasks—like caring for your home or keeping organized—they learn the importance of responsibility.

2. **Prioritize Tasks**: Show how you prioritize and manage responsibilities effectively. Verbalize your to-do lists or plans to encourage your child to apply similar strategies in their own lives.

2. Share Responsibilities

1. **Involve Children in Household Tasks**: Engage your child in household responsibilities, allowing them to see you actively participating in chores or work. Explain the importance of each task in contributing to a functioning household.
2. **Set an Example during Conversations**: Practice effective communication during family discussions. Encourage children to express their ideas while validating their opinions. This environment teaches values such as respect and cooperation.

Cultivating a Growth Mindset

A growth mindset is the belief that abilities and intelligence can be developed through dedication and hard work. Modeling a growth mindset encourages children to embrace challenges and learn from failures.

1. **Emphasize Effort Over Perfection**: Celebrate effort and improvement rather than solely focusing on outcomes. When reflecting on achievements, highlight perseverance, resilience, and the lessons learned along the way.
2. **Share Personal Challenges**: Discuss your own challenges and setbacks. When children see you navigating difficulties and adapting, they develop an understanding that growth comes from facing challenges.

Leading by Example in Everyday Life

1. **Daily Gratitude Practice**: Model gratitude by verbally acknowledging the positive aspects of your day with your child. Encourage them to express gratitude as well, fostering appreciation and positivity.
2. **Healthy Lifestyle Choices**: Demonstrate healthy habits by eating nutritious meals, exercising, and prioritizing self-care. Your commitment to a healthy lifestyle sets a precedent for your child.
3. **Continuous Learning**: Show enthusiasm for learning new things, whether it's picking up a new hobby or enrolling in a class. Encourage your child to be curious and open to new experiences.

Conclusion of Chapter 14

Modeling behavior is one of the most potent tools in parenting. By consciously demonstrating positive actions, effective communication, and responsibility, you equip your child with the skills they need to navigate life successfully. The lessons they learn from your example will help shape their character and decision-making for years to come. In the concluding chapter, we will explore the journey to success—nurturing lifelong skills in kids that will serve them throughout their lives.

Chapter 15: The Journey to Success - Nurturing Lifelong Skills in Kids

Nurturing Lifelong Skills: The Journey to Success

The journey to success isn't just about reaching specific goals; it's about cultivating the skills and habits that will serve children throughout their lives. As parents and caregivers, our role in nurturing these essential skills is crucial—after all, we're the guides on this exciting adventure! In this final chapter, we'll explore key lifelong skills that are vital for children's personal, academic, and social success, along with practical strategies to encourage their development.

Key Lifelong Skills to Nurture

What are these invaluable skills? Let's unpack them:

1. **Critical Thinking and Problem-Solving**: In today's complex world, the ability to think critically and solve problems is non-negotiable. Children must learn to analyze situations, evaluate options, and make informed decisions—essentially, becoming mini-analysts of their own lives!

2. **Communication Skills**: Effective communication is more than just speaking—it involves listening actively and empathetically. These skills lay the groundwork for healthy relationships and successful professional interactions.

3. **Emotional Intelligence**: Think of emotional intelligence as the GPS for social navigation. It encompasses self-awareness, empathy, and the ability to manage one's emotions. Children with high emotional intelligence can navigate social landscapes with finesse and handle challenges with grace.

4. **Time Management and Organization**: These skills help kids prioritize, stay organized, and manage their time effectively. As a result, they can balance academic responsibilities with personal interests, setting the stage for future success.

5. **Resilience and Grit**: Life isn't always smooth sailing, and teaching kids to cope with setbacks and adapt to challenges is vital. Resilience empowers them to persevere in the face of difficulties—a crucial component of overall well-being.

6. **Independence and Self-Motivation**: Fostering independence gives children the confidence to take ownership of their decisions and actions, promoting self-motivation and accountability.

Strategies to Nurture Lifelong Skills

Ready to equip your little ones with these super skills? Let's dive into some practical strategies!

1. Encourage Critical Thinking

Help your child flex their mental muscles!

- **Ask Open-Ended Questions**: Instead of seeking straightforward answers, spark conversations with questions like, "What do you think about...?" or

"How would you approach this situation?" This opens up a world of possibilities!

- **Introduce Problem-Based Learning**: Present real-world problems for your child to tackle. Plan a family outing on a budget or organize a community project together. This hands-on approach encourages exploration and creativity.

2. Foster Communication Skills

Let's turn conversations into enriching exchanges!

- **Practice Active Listening**: Model active listening by giving your child your full attention during discussions. Reflect on what they say to show understanding and engagement, making them feel valued.

- **Encourage Storytelling**: Invite your child to share stories about their day or personal experiences. This practice enhances their ability to articulate thoughts and emotions clearly—who doesn't love a good story?

3. Develop Emotional Intelligence

Let's build a powerful emotional toolkit!

- **Teach Emotional Vocabulary**: Help your child expand their emotional vocabulary by discussing various feelings. Prompt them to express emotions verbally with questions like, "How did that make you feel?"

- **Role-Play Scenarios**: Use role-playing to practice responses to different social situations. This can be especially helpful for teaching empathy and conflict resolution skills.

4. Promote Time Management and Organization

Time flies when you're having fun, but let's keep it steady!

- **Create Daily Schedules**: Collaborate with your child to create a visual schedule of daily tasks. Whether it's chores, homework, or fun time, checklists can help keep them organized and focused.

- **Set Time Limits for Tasks**: Encourage effective time management by setting reasonable limits for tasks. Use timers so children learn to gauge how long activities should take.

5. Cultivate Resilience and Grit

Time to build some serious character!

- **Model Resilience**: Share stories of your own setbacks—highlight how you coped with adversity and what you learned from difficult experiences. Kids need to see that challenges are a part of life!

- **Encourage a 'Growth Mindset'**: Reinforce the idea that challenges are opportunities for growth. Instead of saying, "I can't do this," shift to "I can't do this yet." This mindset encourages development and perseverance.

6. Nurture Independence and Self-Motivation

Let's help them blossom into independent thinkers!

- **Set Personal Goals**: Encourage your child to set personal goals—be it academic or personal. Help them lay out a plan to achieve those goals and regularly check in on their progress.

- **Provide Choices**: Allow your child to make choices in various areas—like choosing a homework schedule or picking chores. This promotes independence and self-management.

Creating a Supportive Environment

The atmosphere you cultivate at home has a HUGE impact!

- **Foster a Growth Mindset Culture**: Create an environment where effort, learning, and personal growth are celebrated. Praise persistence and creativity—not just success.

- **Encourage Exploration**: Give your child the freedom to explore new activities, hobbies, and interests. This exploration fosters creativity and adaptability—key ingredients for lifelong learning.

- **Create Safe Spaces for Failure**: Normalize failure as a natural part of life. Provide a supportive space for discussing setbacks and learning from them, free from judgment.

The Role of Family and Community

Let's not forget the power of community!

- **Engage in Community Activities**: Involve your child in community service or local events. These activities teach social skills, empathy, and teamwork while reinforcing their connection to the wider world.

- **Establish Family Traditions**: Create traditions that promote personal achievement and growth—whether celebrating educational milestones or reflecting on accomplishments together.

Conclusion of Chapter 15

Nurturing lifelong skills in children is a continuous journey that requires patience, intention, and proactive engagement. As parents and caregivers, we hold the unique opportunity to guide our children along their path to success by modeling positive behaviors, encouraging exploration, and fostering resilience. By equipping them with the essential skills needed to navigate life's challenges, we empower our kids to grow into confident, capable individuals ready to face a world brimming with possibilities.

Final Thoughts
(and a quick favor to ask!)

As you embark on this journey of parenting, remember that every small step counts. By implementing the methods outlined in this book, you can foster an environment where children feel heard, respected, and motivated to cooperate. Whether helping defiant kids listen or encouraging lazy kids to work, the skills and strategies shared will serve you well on your journey as a parent.

The journey to success is not just about the destination; it is about nurturing a love for learning, resilience, and a positive approach to life's challenges. Together, let us empower the next generation to listen, work hard, and embrace the beautiful complexities of life.

Thank you very much for choosing to read my latest book. It would mean the world to me if you could take just a minute and leave an honest review about this book. Much appreciated!